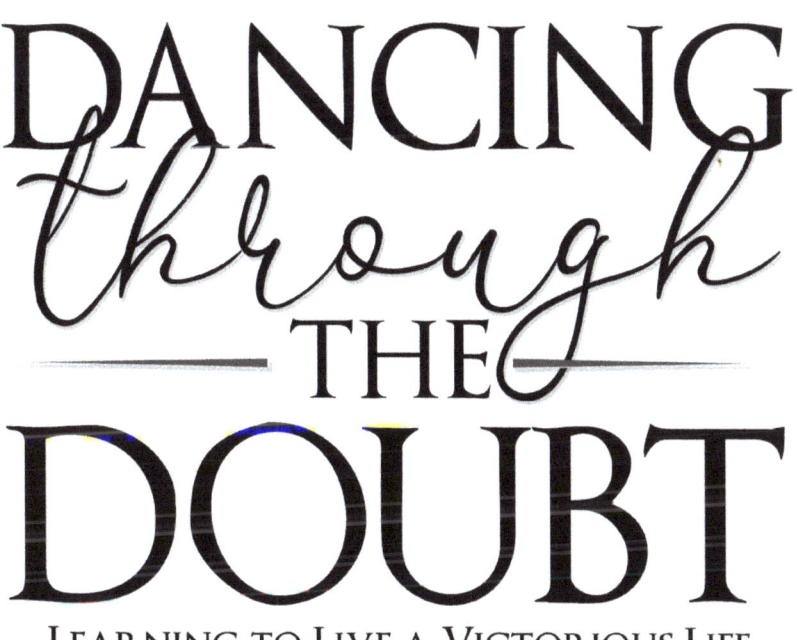

DANCING through THE DOUBT

Learning to Live a Victorious Life

JACQUELINE SAWYER

Copyright © 2021 Jacqueline Sawyer

Unless otherwise indicated, all Scripture quotations are taken from the Holy Bible, New Living Translation, copyright © 1996, 2004, 2015 by Tyndale House Foundation. Used by permission of Tyndale House Publishers, Inc., Carol Stream, Illinois 60188. All rights reserved. "Scripture quotations are from the ESV® Bible (The Holy Bible, English Standard Version®), copyright © 2001 by Crossway, a publishing ministry of Good News Publishers. Used by permission. All rights reserved." Scripture quotations from The Authorized (King James) Version. Rights in the Authorized Version in the United Kingdom are vested in the Crown. Reproduced by permission of the Crown's patentee, Cambridge University Press

All rights reserved. No part of this document may be reproduced or transmitted in any form or by any means, electronic, mechanical, photocopying, recording, or otherwise, without prior written permission of the author.

DANCING THROUGH THE DOUBT
Learning to Live a Victorious Life

Jacqueline Sawyer
dancersawyer@yahoo.com

ISBN 978-1-949826-28-9
Printed in the USA.
All rights reserved

Published by: EAGLES GLOBAL BOOKS | Frisco, Texas
In conjunction with the 2021 Eagles Authors Course
Cover & interior designed by DestinedToPublish.com

Book Dedication

I dedicate this book to my niece Yvette; my nephews Joseph III, Marcello, and Isaac; grand-nieces Jada and Jalyn; and grand-nephews Joshua, Miles, and Maceo. You inspire me every day to be a motivating force in your lives.

Acknowledgments

This book writing journey took me along a pathway where I earned a deeper level of spiritual maturity. Moving past self-doubt and trusting in the power of God to transform my thinking was possible because of many caring people who nurtured me through the process.

First and foremost, I am grateful for the loving memory of my mother, Dorothy Holloway Sawyer Campbell, who laid the foundation for my thirst for knowledge and love of God.

Jakki Hunt, my spiritual mother, who prays and stands in the gap for me every step of the way.

All of the Morning Intercessory Prayer Warriors, Times Square Church Women's Fellowship, National Liturgical Dance Network, and Dance For Joy Ministries members who daily pray and encourage me.

Lastly, I am grateful for my siblings, Gwendolyn Blackwell and Joseph Sawyer Jr., for always being available to love and support me.

Table of Contents

Prologue vii

Chapter 1: F.A.I.T.H.
    Fully Accepting I Am To Heal Me 1

Chapter 2: B.E.
    Blessed Eternally 13

Chapter 3: H.E.A.R.T.
    Heaven's Eternal Answer Revealing
    And Restoring Truth 25

Chapter 4: K.N.O.W.
    Kingdom Knowledge Overflowing
    Within Me 33

Chapter 5: F.E.A.R.
    False Evidence Appearing Real 39

Chapter 6: H.O.P.E.
    Hallelujah Our Praise to God
    Encourages Us 45

Chapter 7: G.A.N.G.S.
   God's Army Nurturing
   Greatness Supernaturally 49

Chapter 8: M.I.N.D.
   Merciful Intuition Nurturing Destiny........ 55

Chapter 9: M.O.M.
   Ministry Of Movement 59

Cited Sources 65

Prologue

"A journey of a thousand miles begins with a single step" – Lao Tzu. This saying teaches that even the longest and most difficult ventures have a starting point. The journey I am sharing with you forced me out of my procrastinating comfort zone and catapulted me into a season of deep introspection, evaluation, and realization that I desperately needed intimacy with God to reveal answers for my troubled soul.

How and where could I begin to get to the root of my spiritual weaknesses? What would I have to do to be free from the fear, doubt, and unbelief that has plagued my life at every pivotal decision-making moment? Confronting the truth about myself and admitting I did not have a relationship with my Creator God exposed the reality: I did not really know Him.

My first step in developing an intimate conversation with God started with a heartfelt prayer: "Lord, have mercy on me. I know I've been operating more on my feelings than trusting and obeying your will and way. I want to surrender my entire life completely over to you and empty myself out and be filled by your presence. I want to know you, God."

Many truths were unveiled to me over a period of being still, listening, and journaling every nugget of wisdom from God's word spoken directly into my heart. I invite all who read this book to experience my journey to acknowledge that in the process of becoming who we want to be, it will require going through varied obstacles to get to our Promised Land.

1

F.A.I.T.H.

Fully Accepting I Am To Heal Me

The most challenging stage of my development was adolescence. Transitioning from childhood to becoming an adult was fraught with so many unknowns. Looking back over those years between the ages of twelve and eighteen, I realize there was a battle going on in my mind that became a permanent part of my daily thinking. Issues with accepting some of my physical changes and rejecting others caused me to feel inadequate in my relationship with the opposite sex. This led to my behavior of seeking acceptance.

My first male relationship was with my father, of whom I was deathly afraid. My father was critical and unaccepting of anything less than perfection. I needed to be accepted by my father but always felt I was never "good enough." No one ever explained to me how to be all I could be.

Both of my parents valued education, and I did my best to make them proud of my academic achievements. Neither of them completed high school: my mother attended school up to the sixth grade, and my father completed ninth grade. Being able to graduate and go to college would fulfill a dream for my parents, and hopefully I would then be accepted as "good enough."

In 1970, I was accepted with a full scholarship to Smith College, a private liberal arts women's college, which was quite an achievement. I was the first and only member of my family to attend college, and the expectations were high. Adjusting to college life instantly made me more aware of questioning myself. Leaving a big cosmopolitan city like New York and settling into the quaint New England town of Northampton, Massachusetts, presented a plethora of concerns about being "good enough."

Attending Smith meant pursuing a career in theatre arts and being immersed in the discovery of my artistic voice. The academic rigor and endless hours of studio training instilled a tenacity to become "good enough." I was ill prepared for the level of acumen expected of me to write, which caused me to doubt my ability to succeed in academia. However, my saving grace was the dance, choreography, and performances throughout my undergraduate years, which turned my life around. I finally realized the power of the arts to open all the creativity locked inside of a young African American girl from Harlem, New York City.

Navigating through the expectations of my parents, teachers, and peers caused undue stress, which led me to become a compulsive overeater. I did not anticipate handling my fears, my doubts, or my thoughts of inadequacy with food. It was almost a double-edged scenario of needing food to survive, yet stuffing down my feelings of low self-esteem with unhealthy choices. Only in hindsight did I realize I justified overeating as an acceptable vice, far better than drugs or alcohol. The long-term effect of rarely speaking my true feelings for fear of being rejected planted seeds of people-pleasing – a real spirit-robber.

Gaining seventeen pounds in my freshman year as a dance major was also the beginning of a form of self-sabotage. Because studying dance education did not require a specific body type, my weight was not a factor in my dance training. I continued to excel in my creativity and was eventually recognized as a committed dancer who garnered the attention of a large Five College audience to support my senior year choreography performance.

Graduating from Smith College established a firm awakening within my spirit. I was born to dance, and however I could use this talent to express myself and impact others to release a joy of movement in their lives would be my mission.

Little did I realize that the academic study of dance is very different from professional training. Upon my return to NYC, this stark reality became evident while attending Dance Theatre of Harlem. The rigorous demands of classical ballet overshadowed the modern dance training I received in college. All the confidence I gained as a modern dancer/choreographer was now being challenged by the relentless demands I put on myself to hurry up and become a ballerina. The expectation to become svelte, achieve a perfect turn-out, and balance my body in countless positions of leg extensions drove me even deeper into compulsive eating.

This focus on my outward appearance was never an issue before embarking on a path to becoming a professional dancer. Daily looking at myself in the mirror during dance classes unfortunately became more about comparing myself to peers rather than critiquing my own progress. Old emotional thoughts about being "good enough" began to resurface and gave way to the fear of rejection, which slowly ate away at my creative voice as an artist. All of these negative thoughts provided an environment for depression to take root, and I sought comfort in junk food.

During my first year back in NYC, I was simultaneously training at DTH and attending Columbia University Teachers College to earn a Master of Arts degree in Dance and Dance Education. For me, academic settings foster a sense of self-discovery, acceptance of my viewpoints, and encouragement. I balanced studying dance during the day and going to college in the evening. My left brain and right brain were fully engaged as I worked on my master's thesis and slowly regained hope for mental stability.

The discomfort I experienced in my mind reflected my soul's need for spiritual healing, but I ignored the tugs of God to seek Him for answers. I relied on my parents, teachers, and peers to define my identity based on their expectations of my achievements. It never occurred to me that I needed to inquire of God for guidance. After all, I gave my life to Christ at twelve years old, attended church regularly, sang in the Inspirational choir, danced for special services, participated in Sunday school, and diligently gave financial offerings. What more did I need to do for spiritual homeostasis? When would I be "good enough" for my parents, Dance Theatre of Harlem, Columbia, or my peers? How could I embrace all of me without needing approval from others?

Despite the emotional turmoil, I was able to recognize the need to evaluate my academic and professional training as it pertains to future employment. Up to this point, I still lived at home with little financial responsibilities. Upon graduation with a Master of Arts in Dance and Dance Education, I needed to confront my career choices as a dance educator or professional performing artist.

Mistake #1, in hindsight, was that I neglected to see the bigger picture. I was so focused on my immediate desire to be a dancer that I did not consider the cost to achieve the goal. The lifestyle of an artist is fraught with uncertainty, rejection, and financial instability, yet I allowed my passion to supersede logic. Even though teaching dance full-time would provide income to pay for additional professional training, headshots, dancewear, and housing, it would interfere with my availability to audition. So, I decided instead to continue professional training, audition, and teach part-time with no health benefits.

Years of temporary dance performance opportunities never fulfilled my spirit. The doubts about my adequacy to be a concert dancer propelled me to audition for Broadway, film, and television, where I was expected to sing, dance, and act. More classes, more money, more fears increased as rejection after rejection caused me to once again ask myself, "Am I 'good enough' to succeed?"

Looking back over my career choices without relying on God as the source of my decision-making process caused me to continue fixating on my external and neglecting my internal. In order to maintain the discipline of dance through my doubt, I discovered a regimen of intense physical exercises to prevent injury, increase stamina, and fortify spinal alignment called Joseph Pilates Muscle Contrology. My whole outlook on mastering maximum mental and physical conditioning was revolutionized by the adroit Pilates master teacher Kathleen Stanford Grant.

In exchange for classes, KSG began to train me as an assistant, and I learned everything she could teach me about the Pilates system. My awareness of the importance of mental preparation through imagery improved my ability to be centered and in rhythmic control of my breathing. These skills dramatically affected my performance level, thereby increasing my chances to become a working artist.

Little did I know how God was orchestrating, choregraphing, laying a foundation for me to become a teacher. In spite of my superficial relationship with my Creator, He knew what I was yet to learn. His will, His way, His timing is not always evident in the natural, but revelation knowledge is available to anyone seeking Him for the answers to life's mysteries. What was the purpose for gaining more skills? Why was I subjecting myself to countless audition rejections? When would I become "good enough" to get a full-time performing job? What more could I do to succeed?

My first major encounter with functional depression (just going through the motions of daily activities) occurred right before I turned thirty years old. I had to face the facts that all my efforts to become a paid performing artist were not sealing the deal, and it was a hard pill to swallow. Confronting my emotional turmoil created within me a mental dystopia perspective on life, which was an outright lie. All of my academic and professional achievements gave me options to pursue a fruitful future. But I could not accept, would not entertain any logical options. Putting off the fulfillment of my goal to be a performing artist would be another admission of my inadequacies.

The battlefield of the mind is where I would submit to countless fears, doubts, and double-mindedness conversations. My mind was like an old-fashioned washing machine, beating the contents in the tub back and forth until the final spin would drain everything dry. Daily I would wake up exhausted from sleepless nights of trying to figure out how to get out, get through the nightmare of not feeling "good enough."

Because of the solid physical regimen of Pilates, dance classes, and teaching, I was able to wear a mask of holding it all together. But in reality, day by day, my spirit was disintegrating from a lack of God's nutrition, His presence and intimacy. The sheer determination not to give up or throw in the towel was fueled by my daily physical routine that kept me on a performance-based lifestyle of self-effort.

Attempting to live a Christian life as a performing artist caused many problems reminiscent of how I felt when my parents would say "you should know better." The word "should" developed a behavioral response where any self-correction was guided by a critical spirit of perfectionism. Trying to live up to the standards of a concert dancer or theatrical performer took a toll on my emotions. The fear of failure, anxiety, and depression was stifling my ability to express my true sense of not being in control of my circumstances.

Living on a performance treadmill affected my mental stability. I became a chronic worrier, developing low self-esteem and a negative attitude toward myself for not being as good as other performers. Big mistake comparing myself to others – as a result, I became a champion of self-condemnation. Depending on the approval of other people to accept me, when I was unable to accept myself, kept me in bondage to my fears of rejection.

Food became my refuge, and the compulsion to stuff down my feelings turned into a disease of compulsive overeating. My relationship with food was handled in the extremes. When stressed, I overate, then felt guilty and fasted. There was no balance in my diet, and I found myself in a state of desperation. Since I had discovered a physical regime to maintain my dancing skills, surely there must be a method to take control of my eating behavior. Where could I find the answers to handle my food addiction?

Auspiciously, while performing in a play at the AMAS Repertory Theatre, I observed an actress intentionally eating her daily lunch with a nutritional discipline that I desired. Upon asking her to divulge her secret of eating control, she did not answer my question but instead invited me to an Overeaters Anonymous meeting. Without hesitation, I agreed to meet her and get all the practices to achieve a healthier balance in my dietary needs.

Every individual who chooses to enter Overeaters Anonymous goes through a twelve-step program, picks a sponsor, and attends daily/weekly sessions to support the transition from eating disorder to balanced food management. The program states: "Our way of life, based on these twelve steps and twelve traditions, has brought us physical, emotional and spiritual healing, that we don't hesitate to call miraculous. What works for us will work for you, too" (*Overeaters Anonymous*).

Still unaware of the hand of God upon me, I would learn and eventually share lessons about compulsive overeating. I attended meetings because I was exhausted by the effects of yo-yo dieting. My prior record as a disciplined student gave me the foundation to pursue the O.A. proven method of food control. Afterall, whether I agreed with the program or not, my dancer body was at stake.

Who knew the great lengths God would go to make me aware of His unconditional love for me through the O.A. program? The introduction to what I thought was a diet became a life-long process of admitting that I am powerless over people and circumstances.

My initial motivation to confront the self-sabotaging effects of my eating disorder changed when I realized my negative emotions were the real culprit hindering my self-acceptance. Step four of the program required me to make a searching and fearless moral inventory of myself. "Wait a minute – I came to O.A. for nutritional guidance. not evaluation of my moral character!" I thought. But God orchestrated another divine intervention in an O.A. meeting, not at church service.

The working through the twelve steps heightened my awareness that I hungered for unconditional acceptance in a relationship with my heavenly Father that I never experienced with my earthly father. Confronting this spiritual awakening began my journey of increasing my faith through recommitting myself to walk by faith and not by sight. This meant turning my complete will and life over to the guidance of God.

"Train up a child in the way he should go: and when he is old, he will not depart from it" (Proverbs 22:6 KJV). My Christian upbringing has been a strong foundation in the development of my moral character. Learning about godly behavior was my first step in making a choice about the kind of life I wanted to live and the kind of person I wanted to become. Up to that point, I had leaned on others for understanding of how to apply scriptures to daily living. Overeaters Anonymous had twelve steps to follow, and the Bible has sixty-six books. It was up to me to seek God in prayer for His help.

"And without faith it is impossible to please God, because anyone who comes to him must believe that he exists and that he rewards those who earnestly seek him" (Hebrews 11:6 NIV). Facing my spiritual impasse was a very challenging decision. In order to break free from mental, emotional, and physical turmoil, I had to do something I never did before: talk to God in prayer about everything.

Throughout my life, I have discovered that if I can create an acronym to remember the significance of a word that impacts the way I think, I am better for it. Going to God in prayer is an act of faith, and I needed to make this concept meaningful to me. Acknowledgment of my spiritual brokenness meant I needed internal healing. Upon meditating on what faith means to me, I created the acronym: **F**ully **A**ccepting **I A**m **T**o **H**eal **M**e.

Before praying, I began a practice of exalting and praising God by using the alphabet. For each letter, I would express a term to describe Him (for example, A=Almighty, B=Benevolent, C=Comforter, and so on). Speaking out loud or writing down these characteristics of God strengthened my connection to His Spirit.

Dear Father God, I truly don't know how to handle the emotional imbalance in my life and the reoccurrence of depression. Help me to accept the changes necessary from your perspective and reveal to me the beliefs I have that are contributing to my despair. Restore my hope, joy, and praise unto you. I am desperate for your presence. Amen. (Adapted from Psalm 42:5 KJV.)

2

B.E.

Blessed Eternally

The first step in seeking answers most often starts with the admission of needing help. Clearly, trying to fix myself in my own strength was not very effective. I made a decision to do whatever it would take to release myself from the bondage of a poor self-image and negative thoughts through in-depth Bible studies. It is said that "the teacher appears when the student is ready," and I was ready.

My introduction to seriously investigating what goes on in my mind was found in the book *Battlefield of the Mind* by Joyce Meyer, who challenged me to think about my thinking. What type of mental conversations did I have with myself? How did I talk about the way I looked or felt on a daily basis? Where did my identity come from? Who was my cheerleader? Who was my worst enemy? Did I believe God loves me? Did I love myself? It was embarrassing to admit that I had really never focused on how my thinking affected my emotions or behaviors.

The resistance to accepting my part in "stinking thinking" manifested procrastination in many areas of my life. I started making excuses for not being adequate as a performer or teacher for fear of failure, when in reality, it was a fear of succeeding and of the expectation to do better.

Submitting myself to the process of intentionally listening to God was extremely difficult. Being able to silence the cacophony of thoughts swirling around in my mind required steadfastness. I was asking myself to do what I constantly asked my students to do when teaching dance in a huge gymnasium simultaneously shared with a physical education class. The noise of fifty students on both sides of the gym with constant whistle-blowing and cheering challenged my dance students to make a commitment to give me their undivided attention. Learning how to filter my voice through the noise and not get distracted from what I was instructing them to do increased their ability to hear what was most important.

I now had to put this into practice, distilling my thoughts so I would be in a position to hear from God. To get a deeper understanding, I chose this scripture to focus on by meditating upon each word: *"Be still, and know that I am God: I will be exalted among the heathen, I will be exalted in the earth"* (Psalm 46:10 KJV).

Focusing on the word "be" caused me to reflect on who I am as a person. What did I think about myself? The old negative thoughts started to arise, but God began to speak into my heart and make me aware through an acronym for "be": Blessed Eternally. My obedience to being still in His presence began to shift my attention from my poor self-image to His description of who I am in His sight:

- Glory to God for reminding me that I have Christ in me, *"the hope of glory"* (Colossians 1:27 KJV).
- I am God's child, for I am born again of the incorruptible seeds of *"the word of God, which liveth and abideth for ever"* (1 Peter 1:23 KJV).
- I am a new creation in Christ (2 Corinthians 5:17).
- I am blessed (Deuteronomy 28:1-14).
- I am victorious (Revelation 21:7).
- I am more than a conqueror (Romans 8:37).
- I am free from condemnation (Romans 8:1).
- I am healed by the stripes of Jesus (1 Peter 2:24).

All of these scriptures and many more began to transform my thinking. Learning how to become sensitive to the Holy Spirit speaking to my spirit increased my intimacy with God. Every day, I spoke these truths out loud to strengthen my identity in Christ. Now I needed to search the Bible and find examples of how other people relied on God to transform their lives. Accepting my state of depression as a Christian was very difficult. I spoke over myself God's truths about me, but it did not automatically set me free from the bondage of years of oppressive thinking. Who or what could I identify with in the Bible to guide my journey to liberty?

The Israelites' story of being enslaved for nearly 400 years in Egypt paralleled how I viewed my state of mind at that time. I felt in bondage to everyone else's perception of who I am and desperately needed to discover how to be liberated. Feelings of hopelessness increased as I gave into beating up on myself, reminiscent of the slave master's whip. Years of mistreatment penetrated the Israelites' souls but could not strip them of their faith. They believed somehow their God would send them a deliverer, and He did. His name was Moses.

Knowing that God is no respecter of one person over another, I began to get a glimmer of hope that He would send me help. After all, I was a faithful dedicated student in dance, academics, and now Bible study. I came across a book of prayers and poetry called *God's Unchanging Hands* written by Monie D. Broadus. As I read the author's foreword describing how this book was written during a time of suffering and depression, I knew it was no accident that I had found it. She expressed how she experienced trials like Job, and walked with Moses and Joshua to cross the Jordan in her life.

"Aha," I thought, "she sounds like me and what I'm confronting in my life right now." I could identify with her process of praying for God's will first, by waiting and watching with spiritual eyes for godly direction. Broadus warns that feelings get in the way of asking God for guidance. "Lord, have mercy on me," I prayed. "I know I've been operating more on my feelings than trusting and obeying your word, God. I want to surrender my entire life completely over to you and empty myself out. I do not want to be like the children of Israel going around and around for forty years in the wilderness, never crossing over Jordan into the Promised Land."

Reflecting on the plight of the Israelites, I asked myself some questions: What kind of mindset and behavior would I have after years of oppression? How would I respond to being set free? How will I adapt to desert life? What challenges will I face in the wilderness? How will I face impossible obstacles? Could I maintain unshakable faith in the pursuit of reaching the Promised Land?

I believe each phase of my coming out of bondage is similar to what most people will eventually experience in their maturation to adulthood. Discovering who you are is a process of shedding many childhood experiences that no longer benefit you as an adult. Seeking out our purpose takes many twists and turns, trials and errors, failures and successes. Setting goals to be attained gives us measurable strategies for reaching our Promised Land destination.

I sought God's help, and He revealed to me that studying the character of Joshua would be a perfect example of unshakable faith in the face of adversity. Joshua served alongside Moses with thousands of Israelites who came out of Egypt and walked through the Red Sea and into the wilderness by faith.

The objective was to get to the Promised Land filled with the hope of a better life. God knew there would be many giants and battles for them to overcome before reaching their destination. Confronting these seemingly insurmountable challenges would require a mindset of a faithful commitment to the Lord, which Joshua exemplified.

God chose Joshua to lead the Israelites over the Jordan River into the Promised Land after the death of Moses. Joshua was commanded by God: *"Only be thou strong and very courageous, that thou mayest observe to do according to all the law, which Moses my servant commanded thee: turn not from it to the right hand or to the left, that thou mayest prosper whithersoever thou goest"* (Joshua 1:7 KJV).

I began to identify with the relationship Joshua experienced with God through the many years of slavery, service to Moses, and willingness to step out on faith into a foreign land. My journey through depression was analogous to the travails of Joshua as he embarked upon being a leader.

Like Joshua, I needed to believe God would be with me every step of the way as I moved into the foreign territory of "thinking about my thinking." It took many years for the Israelites to shed their slave mentality through the difficult times in the wilderness. Similarly, it would be a long process for me to weed out years of fear, doubt, and unbelief that had kept me in bondage.

God showed favor toward Joshua because of his obedience, and as a result, he prospered in all his ways. Learning to obey

God meant I needed to trust Him and believe when He says, *"Fear thou not; for I am with thee: be not dismayed; for I am thy God: I will strengthen thee; yea, I will help thee: yea, I will uphold thee with the right hand of my righteousness"* (Isaiah 41:10 KJV).

I wanted to start prospering in my career choices as I trusted God to help transform my thinking. I decided to lay hold of God's promises to create a strong foundation for me to walk by faith and not by sight. Embracing the word gradually broke through the walls of my unbelief.

In preparation for any performance, I would warm up my body to prepare my muscles for action. All my dance training supported my ability to move gracefully across the stage. My singing lessons taught me how to breathe properly and project the sound of each note. My acting classes helped me dig deep into the emotional content of a scene and become a variety of different characters. All of these skills merged in the 1980s when I was chosen to be the Lady in Green in a bus and truck tour of *For Colored Girls Who Have Considered Suicide/When The Rainbow Is Enuf* by Ntozake Shange.

Being on tour in this play was equivalent to facing giants in a foreign land. Traveling from city to city in a van for long stretches of time with irregular eating times wrecked havoc on my dancer's body. The pressure to be ready to perform on a different size stage each night with limited rehearsal time challenged my ability to perform with confidence. I opened the play with a solo dance that set the tone for the show.

I convinced myself that I had to be perfect, which led to unnecessary emotional and mental stress.

How was I going to manage my inner turmoil? Resorting to compulsive overeating to soothe my pent-up feelings would negatively affect my dancing body weight and jeopardize my level of performance. I knew I was beginning to emotionally unravel as the temptation to eat my stashed food in the back of the van was increasing. I needed immediate intervention and asked our stage manager if we could stop for an early dinner, to which everyone in the cast agreed. I went straight to a phone booth in the restaurant to contact someone in Overeaters Anonymous to help me while the cast was eating.

The O.A. contact person in Arizona was available to speak with me and listen to my anxious thoughts. She told me that on that day, she had just celebrated eight years of abstaining from compulsive overeating. If I wanted to be liberated from my compulsion, I must be wiling to let go of the food and trust God to help me. She read a poem about the cunning ways addiction to food could prevent me from being the best person I was meant to be.

I stood in the phone booth listening, crying, and hoping I would be able to release my urge to stuff down my feelings with food and make it to the next performance. I went out to the van and threw away all the junk food I had hidden in the back-seat area. With tears flowing, I knew I would not be able to face the cast and risk any questions about my absence during the meal.

Right down the road from the restaurant, I saw a large open field where I was drawn to cry out loud for strength from God in my despair. I just could not take it anymore; I was living in constant fear and anxiety of my weaknesses being exposed. I lifted my hands up to the heavens in total surrender to God. I admitted I was powerless over food and needed Him to restore my unmanageable life with peace of mind.

In the middle of the field, God met me where I was standing and lovingly whispered to me the same promise He gave to the people of Israel and Joshua in Isaiah 41:10. He personalized it for me: "Do not be afraid, Jacqueline, for I am with you. Jacqueline, do not be dismayed, for I am your God who will strengthen and help you." In my desperation to have God intervene on my behalf, I took a step of faith that I had never before put into practice. My act of surrendering gave me a peace that surpassed all of my understanding. My encounter with God increased my trust in Him to supply all of my needs. I began to search the scriptures to be reminded of how obedience to God's word would strengthen my relationship with Him.

"Somebody almost walked off with all of my stuff" was the first line I spoke as the Lady in Green in the play. It was a very long monologue that took hours of memorizing to learn and execute with feeling. The repetition of speaking the words over and over out loud helped me to remember each sentence with conviction. I decided to apply my memorization skills to scriptures that would help me transform my thinking to God's way of thinking.

The practice of writing specific memory verses on file cards, meditating on each word, and repeatedly speaking the scriptures out loud increased my faith and obedience to God. I chose two verses in Proverbs to start dissecting and meditating upon for obedience: *"Trust in the Lord with all thine heart; and lean not unto thine own understanding. In all thy ways acknowledge him, and he shall direct thy paths"* (Proverbs 3:5-6 KJV).

The New Webster's Comprehensive Dictionary defines trust as "confidence in a person or thing because of the qualities one perceives or seems to perceive in him or it." My renewed desire to have a personal intimate relationship with God motivated me to reflect on His character. He is the Healer, the Deliverer, the Counselor, the Comforter, and the Protector. His acts of mercy and grace towards me have assured me that I can trust Him with all of my heart.

My willingness to let go of doing things my way has been a gradual process of trial and error. Submitting my will for His way and timing is still a work in progress that requires a lot of patience on my part. The acknowledgment of Him in all my decision-making affirms my expectation that His way is the best pathway for my life.

The commitment to renewing my mind depended on me daily declaring Who I Am in Christ. I practice looking into a mirror and saying, "I am loved, healed, whole, blessed, victorious, confident, grateful, generous, anointed, courageous, and free from condemnation." Personalizing scriptures and creating prayers based on God's word relevant to a specific need helped me to grow in faith and intimacy with God.

Dear Father God, I am trusting you with all of my heart and will not lean on my own understanding. I believe you will help me to stand on your word that says I can do all things through Christ Jesus who strengthens me. I will cast down any thoughts contrary to your truth about me. I will be a doer of your word and not just a hearer. Every day in every way, I surrender my will and life over to you. I love you, Lord, for first loving me, Amen. (Scripture references: Proverbs 3:5-6, Philippians 4:13, 2 Corinthians 10:5, and James 2:22.)

3

H.E.A.R.T.

Heaven's Eternal Answer Revealing And Restoring Truth

Confronting the thoughts in my mind that needed to be changed was going to require a lot of honesty. Quieting the voices in my head could not happen until I asked God for help. It became a necessary practice to talk to Him upon waking and ask for His help to filter out the things in my heart that didn't align with His.

My conversations with God are so precious that I needed to write in my journal to remember that when I seek Him, I will get answers. I began to meditate upon Psalm 139:23 (KJV), *"Search me, O God, and know my heart."* When I started thinking about what it means to search my heart, it led me to ask myself, "Do I really want to know? Am I ready to hear what God finds in me that is not like Him? Have I resisted a thorough investigation of my true nature and, as a result, unintentionally been too prideful to accept the sin and disobedience that gets in the way of confessing to God my struggles in my mind? Lord, I want to stop making excuses and surrender my heart to you." I realized the heart is connected to my thinking, as stated in Proverbs 23:7 (KJV): *"For as he thinketh in his heart, so is he."*

In my journaling, I asked the Lord to reveal to me what He saw in my heart. I asked Him to help me face whatever strongholds I had allowed to reside in my heart and transform my heart of stone to flesh. God responded through an acronym for "heart": Heaven's Eternal Answer Revealing and Restoring Truth.

I believe God knows exactly how to communicate with each person's heart. In my case, He lets me know through acronyms that He has heard my cry for help. Focusing on heaven's eternal answer gave me the assurance that whatever I bring to the Lord as a request, His response will be the truth for my life. He wants me to listen, trust, and obey the process of His restoring my heart.

After the *For Colored Girls* bus and truck tour came to an end, I needed to find new employment. Being on tour prevented me from auditioning for summer productions. What was going to provide me with a source of income to cover dance classes and living expenses? The answer came through one of the *For Colored Girls* cast members offering me a chance to work with children in a teaching position sponsored by New York University.

The ten-workshop curriculum was developed by a theatre-in-education company called the Creative Arts Team. I would teach creative drama lessons with another actor to elementary-aged students from various backgrounds. This was my first attempt at combining drama and movement exercises to introduce spontaneous theatre experiences for children.

My confidence level was being challenged in this new format of teaching. I was more comfortable teaching dance to students who wanted to dance and had a disciplined focus to learn. The children in the creative drama workshops had to be taught in a very short time how to control their bodies and express themselves through various dramatic scenes. The creative drama classes had a mixture of students from various countries, and working with children who spoke English as their second language made me realize how much I needed to be aware of the power of non-verbal communication. I discovered that the way to improve socialization was achieved through creative movement experiences.

The Creative Arts Team offered me a full-time position teaching drama in education to elementary schools across New York City. Once again, I was being led to explore my dance education skills instead of performing full-time. What was God going to do to prepare me for this new adventure?

Stepping out of my comfort zone brought fears to the surface. I began to question my ability to adapt my dance studio teaching skills into a traditional public-school classroom. My saving grace was the Creative Arts Team's format, in which the workshops involved team teaching. The shared responsibility lessened my anxiety and allowed me to gradually trust the flow of lessons between me and my partner.

I had to resist my tendency toward perfectionism as I evaluated the development of my new teaching style. The ability to drown out the voices of my past fears of failure or inadequacy demanded an increase in my faith. God began to reveal to me that I needed His help to let go of the negative images of myself and discover who I am in His sight.

Little by little, spending more time in the presence of God caused me to confront some of my weaknesses. I don't like to admit that I have a critical spirit. I have a tendency to see what is wrong more than what is right. This type of perspective has caused me to beat up on myself, which has hindered stability in my confidence. How was God going to show me the way out of self-condemnation?

Giving thanks with a grateful heart was the beginning of seeing with eyes of faith. God reminded me to write down a gratitude list every day. Everything was important to acknowledge as a blessing from God. Learning to focus on what I have instead of what I lacked slowly transformed my critical spirit. My willingness to be transparent before the Lord is a daily practice of surrendering my heart to become more like Him.

In Overeaters Anonymous meetings, I would hear people say, "God is good orderly direction." During my quiet time with the Lord, the question of who is in control of my life needed to be addressed. I realized I needed to confront my weakness of wanting to be in control.

Team teaching for C.A.T. heightened my awareness that I wanted to be in control in the classroom, and at the same time, God was showing me how little I trusted Him when teaching. I've learned that wanting to be in control while being fearful of trying new things in my life gives me little opportunity to discover or explore new ways of handling creative expression.

Striving for perfectionism fed into my need to be in control. I don't remember thinking in my growing up years that it was okay to fail sometimes. My parents seemed to expect me to always know how to do my best without any criteria to help me evaluate whether I had achieved a set goal. As a result, I got the message to play it safe in making new decisions for my life.

I really did not know how to set expectations for success. My dependency on allowing other people's standards to influence my decision-making process gave me a false image of being in control. My quiet time with the Lord began to reveal that I needed to make a decision as to who was truly in control of my life.

Letting go and letting God be in control is a daily process of learning how to obey His will and His way. My acceptance of being a full-time teaching artist for C.A.T. shifted my focusing from auditioning to improving my pedagogical skills. What was God going to do to transform my heart and mind to align with His plan for my future? How was I going to submit to this change of direction in my life?

The benefits of being a New York University C.A.T. employee included receiving tuition remission for classes offered at the university. I was aware of a Dance Education program in the School of Education for Music and Performing Arts Professions. I decided to enroll in some of the dance classes to maintain my professional skills, but in hindsight, this was a door God was opening for me to combine my love of dance while increasing my knowledge of how to teach in public education.

Learning to trust and obey God to pursue a Ph.D. in Dance and Dance Education from New York University meant facing my thoughts of not being "good enough" all over again. Confronting my fears of failure could only be dealt with in prayer. God had brought me through compulsive overeating one day at a time. I submitted to His way to be the controlling presence in my life and stepped out in faith to discover who I would become as a dance educator.

Dear Father God, I humble myself before you and admit that I needed your guidance to pursue a doctorate. Help me remember all the ways you have been faithful to supply all my needs in the past. Forgive me when I become impatient with the process of growing in faith. Help me to daily acknowledge your goodness by instilling in me an attitude of gratitude. Continue to open the eyes of my heart to see you in the midst of my circumstances as I embark on this new season of my life. I am trusting you, Lord, to help me move beyond my fears, doubts, and insecurities to experience your strength when I am distracted by my negative thoughts that contradict your truth. Thank you for loving me, forgiving me, and drawing me into an intimate relationship with you. Amen.

4

K.N.O.W.

Kingdom Knowledge Overflowing Within Me

Right now as I am writing in 2021, I am being confronted with unbelief. Everything inside of my mind feels like a struggle to focus on the truth of God's word. My emotions are overpowering my faith, and the spirit of oppression is trying to take up residence in my mind.

Learning to silence the lies of the adversary is a daily battle. I have to make a constant effort to stay connected to the source of my strength and remember how God is bigger than my fears. I have to call upon the Holy Spirit to help me remember how God has brought me through to reach where I am now.

Being still in God's presence revealed an acronym for the word "know": Kingdom Knowledge Overflowing Within Me. This was revealed to my spirit in 2019 to help me trust the process of intimacy. I began to reflect on the power of all of God's knowledge stored up inside of me to guide and direct my life. Accepting and taking action on this knowledge has been an uphill battle.

Unbelief hinders the gifts, talents, and abilities God has given me to fulfill my purpose. It is so frustrating to know the truth that has set me free, yet still be experiencing bondage. Without a doubt, I'm being confronted to step out on faith, not my feelings, to overcome unbelief.

I am questioning myself about my relationship with Jesus. Have I fully allowed Him to be Lord over all in my life? What do I need to do to surrender the hurts, pain, and disappointments of my childhood that seem to continue to get in the way of how I view myself? How have I been able to overcome, up to this point in my life?

Taking the first step in unraveling the truth from the lies requires a daily commitment to being honest with myself. Accepting what I believe to be true has determined my actions. Taking full responsibility for my choices in life is uncomfortable at times, because I would have to admit I don't have all the answers.

Only God knows the end from the beginning. Learning to bring all my concerns to Him first is a humbling process. Trusting His timing for the next season in my life is in contrast to the world's way of logic. The willingness to transform my thinking to align with God's will for my life means acknowledging that I will know who I am when I know who He is in totality.

Prayer is essential in my relationship with God. This is an example of journaling my first time of praying to be cleansed in my heart, mind, and body:

Thank you, Lord, for guiding me in my preparation to sit in your presence, purging any thoughts from my mind that would offend you. As I went through my body, I asked for eyes to see spiritually, my hearing ears to blot out any negativity, that my mouth would reject unhealthy foods and my tongue would speak lovingly, kindly, gently, with uplifting words to myself and others. Help me, Lord, to discern the inward condition of my heart instead of focusing on the outward appearance of things. Help me retain any freedom from bondage (such as compulsive overeating). Lord, let me not forget anything you have set me free from. I trust my time with you today is moving me into total surrender to you and letting go of feelings that hinder my stepping out in faith.

This journal entry prayer was written a couple of years ago in 2017 when I had forgotten to persist in a daily practice of being still with God. The result of neglecting consistent intimacy with God gradually weakened my faith and caused me to rely on my own strength, not His. I need to remember God's truth: *"Casting down imaginations, and every high thing that exalteth itself against the knowledge of God, and bringing every thought into captivity to the obedience of Christ"* (2 Corinthians 10:5 KJV).

I have to make a choice to believe by faith and speak over myself: "I am the head and not the tail; I'm above only and not beneath; greater is He that is in me than he that is in the world; and I walk by faith and not by sight."

God sees me as a conqueror/overcomer through Christ's strength in me, not my own. I need to remember I'm still in the process of overcoming and not beat up on myself for having human frailties. In journaling, I'm able to benefit from reflecting on God's voice reminding me that I am *"being born again, not of corruptible seed, but of incorruptible, by the word of God, which liveth and abideth for ever"* (1 Peter 1:23 KJV).

I acknowledge, Lord, nothing can change what is inside of a seed. Everything that you purpose for the seed to become will occur over time. When I invited you into my heart, Jesus, the seed of the word of God of was planted in my heart to grow through the nurturing of the Holy Spirit. My time of silence, stillness, waiting on you is necessary for the seed to take root and fill me with your goodness, kindness, love, faith, courage, wisdom, knowledge, longsuffering, forgiveness, and humility, and for your purpose for my life to be known to me.

Dear Father God, help me every day in every way to turn my will and life over to you. Lord, help me to stand on your word that is the truth about me. Help me to develop a relationship with you that I can depend upon to filter out the lies, condemnation, and doubts. Help me to clarify and identify the parts of my soul that need to be healed. I want to give you all of me – teach me how to surrender. I am determined to go through this brokenness, relying on revelation knowledge from the Holy Spirit one day at a time. Amen.

5

F.E.A.R.

False Evidence Appearing Real

The first time I heard this acronym for "fear" was at an Overeaters Anonymous meeting many years ago. I began to recognize that some of my emotional turmoil in response to "false evidence appearing as real" scenarios was controlling my behavior to confidently move forward in my life.

No one told me I had to be perfect to be loved, valued, or accepted. Yet somehow, in my thinking, the spirit of perfectionism became a stumbling block I could not overcome without God's help. My continual struggle to be "good enough" caused me to doubt myself in everyday decisions, and fearing what people would think of me if I failed led to procrastinating.

There is an antidote to the lies I've told myself about being inadequate, but it is up to me to search, find, and apply God's truths. Therein lies my responsibility to depend on the Holy Spirit to help me become who God says I am.

Learning from the scripture that *"God hath not given us the spirit of fear; but of power, and of love, and of a sound mind"* (2 Timothy 1:7 KJV) reminds me that the source of my fears is the adversary, who is the father of all lies. Whenever I'm tempted to procrastinate because I fear failing, I say to myself, "I will do my best, and God will do the rest."

Remembering that *"perfect love casteth out fear"* (1 John 4:18 KJV) assures me that God's love for me is the foundation for all He has created me to become. I'm constantly under construction one day at a time as I'm being perfected into His image.

During a time of being still in God's presence on January 12, 2019, I wrote in my journal about the Full Armor of God described in Ephesians 6:1-18. I was led to personalize and express my understanding of the importance of God's strategy for me to be protected from the attacks of the adversary. Ephesians 6:10-13 is most important to listen to, because the Lord is giving me direct, concrete, and emphatic commands to prepare me for battle. Be strong in the Lord, Jacqueline, be empowered by your relationship with Him. Put on the full armor; every piece of armor has a specific role that is necessary to defeat the enemy. Remember, if any piece is missing, it allows penetration to my mind, body, and soul resulting in spiritual warfare in heaven and on earth. Resist and stand, guard my ground in the evil day. Recognize that the weapons of my warfare are not carnal but are mighty through God to the pulling down and tearing down of spiritual and mental strongholds. Gird myself (encircle my waist) with truth (Ephesians 6:14).

I began to declare scripture to provide me with power to stand firm (Psalm 23, 27, 139; Philippians 4:6-8). I think about my loins as a place where life begins as the word, the incorruptible seed of God is being planted in my womb to grow roots of steadfastness to adhere to God's righteousness. I put on the Breastplate of Righteousness, asking God to reveal known and unknown sin in my heart so I can repent, confess, and accept correction from God. I put on my feet the Gospel of Peace, so that wherever I walk, the ground will be holy and sanctified. I will bring joy, kindness, and love. I will be consecrated unto the Lord and prepared to face the enemy. I put on the Shield of Faith to extinguish, deflect every fiery dart of the adversary. This part of the armor is where I earnestly pray that God would not allow any weapons formed against me and my family to prosper (Isaiah 54:17). I individually name each family member, friend, and ministry for protection. Today I put on the Helmet of Salvation that protects my mind, will, emotions, imagination, and memories.

God spoke specifically to me about each entity that He would protect through salvation. Never before did I begin to weep the way I did when God spoke into my heart and said: "Give Me your mind, Jacqueline, so I can transform it into the mind of Christ. Allow Me to take control over every thought that is in opposition to My truth and My will. Trust Me to transform your thinking, so My thoughts and visions become yours. Let go of your will, and I will replace it with My will. Allow me to change your attitude, perspective, and behavior to align with My plans for your life. Allow me to handle all of your emotions, for this is necessary to move toward freedom and confidence so you will never again be in bondage to fear, doubt, unbelief, double-mindedness, inadequacy, or rejection. Remember to trust Me with all of your heart. Allow Me to be a part of your imagination – the uncharted territory where anything is possible. Embrace doing new things outside of your comfort zone."

God wants to stir up all the gifts inside of me and use them to help others see Him move in their life. God said to remember:

- How I saved you at twelve years old from following your flesh to instead yield to Jesus Christ as Lord.
- How I delivered you from unhealthy relationships based on physical intimacy which hindered your communication with me.
- How I provided for your academic and artistic education that laid a foundation for your financial security and confirmation of my goodness.
- How I protected you during your time of persecution and isolation at work as an educator.
- How I put new divine friendships in your life.

- How I have drawn you to Dance Ministry and associations with artists who desire to spread the gospel through the arts.
- How I've answered your prayers for intimacy and relish our quiet times together where I hear your heart and you listen to my promises.
- FORGET past hurts, unforgiveness, condemnation, guilt, inadequacy, worry, anxiety, missed opportunities. I am doing a new thing in you.

Remember that the sword of the Spirit is the word of God, and place it on every situation and circumstance. "My word does not go out of my mouth to you and return void to me," thus saith the Lord (Isaiah 55:11). It has been a valuable practice to journal, memorize scriptures to strengthen my faith, and put on the Full Armor of God to protect my thinking.

6

H.O.P.E.

Hallelujah Our Praise to God Encourages Us

Learning to persevere through life's challenges has taught me how trials will test our faith. It seems the hard lessons in my life have taken time to develop and strengthen my character. I experienced the discipline to resist giving up under pressure while working toward a doctoral degree in Dance and Dance Education at New York University.

Over the eleven years 1985-96 it took to complete courses, research, and writing a dissertation, I was simultaneously employed as a full-time dance educator in a New York City public school. The challenge of balancing my teaching responsibilities of training, choreographing, and directing an after-school dance company while attending evening graduate courses required me to step out on faith.

The enormous amount of mental energy necessary to maintain academic excellence and artistic creativity demanded an increase in self-care activities. My tendency to allow myself to feel overwhelmed could easily spiral into negative thinking if I ignored the warning signs of depression.

Once my joy of movement starts to wane, my spirit is alerting me that something is wrong. God has given me the gift of dancing to freely express myself and help others to discover the connection between body, mind, and spirit. The awareness of any spiritual disconnect between me and God drives me to prayer and the word.

My personal relationship with God assures me I can ask Him, *"Why art thou cast down, O my soul? And why art thou disquieted within me? Hope thou in God: for I shall yet praise him, who is the health of my countenance, and my God"* (Psalm 42:11 KJV). Listening for God's answer to our prayers instills within us a hopeful expectancy for the best solution to meet our needs. His reply to me was to embrace the love He has for me by loving all the parts of myself without judgment.

Taking time to listen to what my spirit needed led me to choose faith over worry. Putting my trust in God to help me make the necessary changes to discipline my body, mind, and spirit to work at maximum efficiency meant establishing a routine for a healthier lifestyle.

I made a daily commitment to wake up early to spend time expressing my love for God and praising Him for all He has done for me. I confessed my desire for an increase in my hunger and thirst for His righteousness. I invited the supernatural power of the Holy Spirit to fill me with more of Him and less of me.

Gradually surrendering to the process of being transformed lessened my anxiety of how to handle the challenges of any given day. My spirit directed my mind to meditate on scriptures, messages from devotionals, and lessons revealed through Bible study. Replacing the old ways of thinking and applying God's truth began to restore my joy.

For example, exercising my faith gave me the energy to exercise, dance, and walk two or three miles in the park on weekends. Teaching dance focuses on the physical development of the students, not the teacher. My rigorous schedule did not allow me to take dance classes, but I was determined to stretch every morning after prayer.

My Pilates training helped me create a fifteen-minute exercise routine to maintain abdominal strength and flexibility. I added light weights, elastic bands, and a hand-held pole to increase my range of movement. The combined practice of daily quiet time with the Lord and exercising improved my mental state.

Trusting God as my anchor in the midst of facing the unknown storms of life requires me to see Him in every situation and circumstance. He knew what I needed to continue developing my Christ-like characteristics during my doctoral journey.

One of the requirements for becoming a doctoral candidate was taking an examination of my knowledge of dance history, choreographers, dancers, anatomy, and aesthetics. There were one hundred short answer questions covering dance from the 1700s to the present date in the 1990s. I had studied for months in preparation for the exam, but the set of questions I was given focused more on theatre arts in relation to dance. I was only able to answer eighty of the questions. In my heart, I knew that I could not give up and fail. I prayed for guidance and received a confirmation in my spirit to describe twenty dance history facts that were not on the original exam in the hope that they would be accepted and I could still pass.

The director of the Dance Department said no one had ever added additional answers on the examination. My bold step of faith secured my candidacy for the doctoral program, and my trust in God increased. This was the first among many future unknown challenges I would encounter in my faith walk.

Before committing to spending daily time in prayer, I didn't realize how joy in the Lord was my strength. He wants us to depend on Him and obey. Praising Him for what He provides, and worshipping Him for who He is, encourages me to maintain communion with Him in prayer.

Dear Father God, I know it is impossible to please you without faith. Thank you for putting a confidence in me to speak to the mountains of my emotional turmoil to be removed from my mind. Help me to believe without any doubt that the things I pray for will come to pass. Amen.

— 7 —

G.A.N.G.S.

God's Army Nurturing Greatness Supernaturally

My journey of dancing through my doubts and seasons of depression rarely made me feel I could live a victorious life. Prior to my commitment to increase my time of intimacy with God, I was trying to be self-reliant. My pride prevented me from asking for help, until the moment I realized it was best for me to surrender my weaknesses for God's strength.

In the scriptures it states, *"Iron sharpeneth iron; so a man sharpeneth the countenance of his friend"* (Proverbs 27:17 KJV). Being transparent and vulnerable before the Lord was a preparation for my honest participation in a small women's group Bible study. Listening to other people reveal their personal challenges gave me the confidence to share without being judged. God wanted me to experience the liberty of being myself in a group seeking His word to strengthen our faith. The benefit of studying, discussing, and praying together in a Bible study group over months made me aware of how much I needed to be held accountable for what I say and do in my walk of faith. Confession of my faults was a sign that I was willing to listen for correction.

God began to help me identify specific women within the group to pray with one-on-one. This additional support encouraged me to confront and gradually overcome doubts about my calling in ministry. The importance of having prayer partners is akin to soldiers on a battlefield requesting reinforcement. They are equipped with the word to do battle against the adversary.

Prayer strengthened my decision to use the skills of a dancer to interpret the word of God. The Lord drew me into dance ministry little by little. In the late 1990s, I started studying ballet with Iris Cloud, a former member of Dance Theatre of Harlem, who founded Dance For Joy Ministries. She combined classical and liturgical dance in her teaching and choreography for DFJ's ensemble, where I became a company member.

My focus changed from dance as entertainment to dance glorifying God. Praying and applying scripture to guide choreographic choices was essential in my training as a liturgical dancer. The commitment to minister with DFJ Ministries helped me step out on faith to impact the lives of others.

I embraced the times of fellowship with DFJ for the positive impact it had on my emotional stability. The love, support, and encouragement I received increased my trust in God's timing for the next season of my spiritual growth. He knew I needed to be surrounded with individuals who would dance with me through my doubts about being adequate and pray for godly wisdom in balancing the demands of my personal life.

During my season with DFJ, my father's health began to deteriorate, and I became his caregiver. The constant demands of making decisions for his health care needs was overwhelming. My relationship with my father became strained under the pressure of his expectations of me to be a perfect daughter.

I did not want a spirit of resentment or bitterness to hinder me in assisting with my father's needs. I cried out to the Lord for guidance and was reminded I was not alone. He had already put prayer partners in my life from the Bible study group and DFJ Ministries who would intercede for healing in my relationship with my dad.

In my quiet time, I began to reflect on my prayer partner group doing good work uplifting people to fulfill their purpose. Another acronym formulated in my mind: G.A.N.G.S. = God's Army Nurturing Greatness Supernaturally. How would this concept manifest in my liturgical dance journey as I overcame doubts and seasons of depression?

Expanding my knowledge and understanding of liturgical dance led me to attend a dance conference in 1998 sponsored by the Allen Liturgical Dance Ministry of Greater Allen Cathedral of New York. Classes were offered in a variety of dance techniques, choreography, and leadership in dance ministry. Hundreds of dance ministries participated from around the world.

During a question/answer session, many dance ministry leaders wanted to know if there was a way to stay connected and supported between conferences. Out of this discussion, the National Liturgical Dance Network was founded by Reverend Eyesha Marable, an associate pastor of Greater Allen Cathedral and part of the leadership team of the Allen Liturgical Dance Ministry.

The NDLN "was developed to provide organizational development and leadership training to Christians who participate in, lead, or have a vision to begin liturgical dance ministries at their prospective churches" (*National Liturgical Dance Network*). Reverend Eyesha Marable was a principal dancer with Footprints Dance Company and Forces of Nature Dance Company. Her passion for liturgical dance and sharing the gospel has helped me develop increased intimacy with God through praise and worship.

Membership in NLDN has made me more aware of spiritual warfare. God is providing me with additional prayer partners to intercede for liturgical dance ministries nationally and throughout the world. The possibility of living a victorious life is achievable, one answered prayer at a time.

Dear Father God, thank you for sending me all the support and encouragement from prayer partners to agree with me in prayer as I seek you for wisdom. Thank you for my weaknesses being surrendered to receive your strength. I am grateful for this poem to express how I am letting go.

The way of unlocking years of suppressed feelings has begun with a challenge

To let go and release freely known and unknown emotions inside of me.

Anxiety, fear, doubt has taken up too much of my mind and hindered the blooming of new goals.

But I believe now is the time to spend with you, God, to unlock the truth about who I am and how I truly feel.

— 8 —

M.I.N.D.

Merciful Intuition Nurturing Destiny

One of the valuable lessons I have learned in my seasons of depression is to manage my emotions one day at a time. God's mercy has helped me shift my focus from self-centeredness to being in service to others. He revealed to me that as a dance educator, I had the unique opportunity to help students unlock and express many emotions through the art of dance. My awareness and my students' needs to be accepted for who they are gave me a servant's heart.

In the process of taking the focus off my own feelings of insecurity and being sensitive to the needs of others, I became grateful for opportunities to volunteer and serve. Something happens to me when I reflect on helping others with no expectation of receiving anything for myself.

During the last week of August 2005, Hurricane Katrina devastated parts of Louisiana and Mississippi. The need and call for immediate help from first responders all over the United States was made known. I was sitting in a Sunday morning service at Times Square Church in New York City when I heard a visiting pastor from Alabama make a request for volunteers along with his church and a disaster relief organization called Christ In Action to help the disaster victims.

My first thought was, "What could I do to help?" The pastor said we could all use our two hands and two feet. My next concern was my responsibility to return to teaching the first week of September. This was the first time I experienced a strong desire to volunteer and be part of an organization that "serves those who cannot help themselves in a disaster situation." After much prayer, I decided to take a few days off from work and prepare to face the many unknown conditions I would encounter in Gulfport, Mississippi.

Interestingly, no thoughts of doubt or inadequacy hindered my willingness to trust God and serve. There was a liberty in my spirit to help in whatever capacity I was given. My first job assignment was to clean and maintain supplies for all portable toilets at the relief site. This area was located on church grounds where people came to be fed hot meals and receive clothing, toiletries, and information to help rebuild their lives.

There were many children who needed their attention to be distracted from the devastation. I began to engage them in some movement games, exercises, and storytelling. The teenagers wanted to help in collecting trash and the fallen tree limbs scattered throughout the neighborhood. I was very grateful to help them find a purpose for part of their day.

The impact of helping others who had lost everything gave me a deeper attitude of gratitude for all God has done in my life. Looking into the faces of disaster victims caused me to acknowledge how God's will, not mine, would be done. He knew my mind needed to be transformed from doubting my abilities to trusting Him to provide the peace to manage my emotions.

The acronym M.I.N.D. = Merciful Intuition Nurturing Destiny came to me during my quiet time with God. He knew the battle in my mind and what it would take to change my perspective about myself. He daily nurtures me through His word as I seek Him to be equipped to fulfill my destiny.

Dear Father God, I thank you for the patience you have with me to yield to your will and your way for my life. Thank you for giving me a heart to serve and share your love with others. Thank you for transforming my mind from the darkness of stinking thinking to the light of your joy, peace, and unconditional love. I am thankful to be aware that you will never leave me or forsake me as I go through the process of spiritual growth for your glory. Amen.

— 9 —

M.O.M.

Ministry Of Movement

My many years as a dance educator, teaching hundreds of students, have given me great joy. I have witnessed the transformation of a student's body, mind, and spirit through movement exploration. It increased my awareness of the power of positive statements. The repetition of speaking encouraging words over my students as they conquered dance combinations instilled in them the confidence to embrace moving out of their comfort zones.

I realize the importance of being a cheerleader for my dance students. The acknowledgment of their improved physical abilities motivated them to work harder. I observed a change of attitude and focus from mediocrity to excellence in their dance performance. My consistent verbal reminders of achievement helped my dance students accept the individual uniqueness of their bodies.

The Lord has impressed upon me the importance of learning how to be a cheerleader for myself. It seems to be easier for me to encourage others to reach their full potential than to acknowledge my own personal achievements. During my quiet time in the presence of God, He reminds me of how He sees me growing in confidence, and that with Him, I am enough.

I begin my day rejoicing about the goodness of God to provide the breath of life as I awake. The physical awareness of my vital organs sustaining bodily functions, and knowing no hurt, harm, or danger attacked me during the night, fuels my praise of Him. The consistent practice of communicating with the Holy Spirit prepares me to hear God's direction for my day and to acknowledge my achievements, big or small.

Encouraging myself with scriptures fortifies my spirit to believe, by faith, that whatever God has called me to do, He will equip me to achieve. Sometimes I create songs from scriptures to motivate me out of the doubts in my mind. I begin to dance my prayers and worship the Lord. I lift up my hands and invite the presence of God to fill me up.

Every new season in my spiritual journey causes me to sing a song representing how God has brought me through a battle in my mind. I remember hearing these words in a song: "I went to the enemy's camp and took back what he stole from me." I would declare out loud, "I am taking back my joy in the Lord who strengthens me, I am taking back my peace of God that surpasses all of my understanding, I am taking back my health because by His stripes I was healed, and I am taking back my mind to think on things above and not below."

The impact and power of dancing has given me an awareness that I was communicating with the Spirit of God to express my true feelings. The releasing of positive energy flowing through every part of my body, touching nerve endings, vital organs, and blood flow, has produced in me a vibrancy to move with strength. I am grateful to God for giving me the opportunity to become a liturgical dancer expressing His glory.

In my previous years as a dance educator, I had sought ways to bring all the elements of dance together into a comprehensive dance curriculum for my students. I visualized a symbol of an open umbrella with many spokes representing all the benefits of a dance experience. This symbol became a thought God gave me in the acronym M.O.M. = Ministry Of Movement.

At the time I received the acronym, I did not yet realize that God was a seed in my spirit not to rely only on my academic and professional training in dance to teach me how to move. He wanted His Spirit living inside of me to guide how, when, and where I moved. Learning that liturgical dance is a ministry to evangelize increased my desire to for deeper intimacy and healing in my soul.

Reflecting on my journey through my doubts about becoming all God created me to be, I can see that it took me in and out of periods of darkness. My times of intimacy with God provided a light to help me navigate a way to handle conflict and decision-making. I am grateful for my awareness that my imperfections do not make me inadequate, but more reliant on God's truth.

Admitting to the battles in my mind was humbling but necessary for me to grow in my faith. If I was going to dance through my doubts, I would to need to take the transformative steps with God leading me all the way.

Writing about my journey has caused me to relive how God brought me through my fears of rejection, failure, and feeling "not good enough." I wanted to share the faithfulness of God to dispel my negative thoughts. He kept me moving forward in His word to trust the process of surrendering my will for His will to be done in my life.

The steps I took to bring me closer to God required me to believe that He always wants what is best for me. Uncovering the root of my spiritual weakness began with a heartfelt prayer of surrender and admission that I wanted to know Him. God revealed to me how the battle in my mind began during my adolescent years. He saw how my need for self-acceptance and validation that I was "good enough" would be satisfied as I spent time in His presence.

Intimacy with God empowered me to let go of my fear of rejection and perfectionism. God used challenging circumstances in my relationships, work, and ministry to confront what needed to be changed in my heart. Worrying about fulfilling the expectations of others is no longer my concern. I do not have to be perfect to be used by God.

Intimacy with God increased my ability to persevere and resist giving up in the face of adversity. Sitting still in His presence builds trust, gives peace, provides guidance, and strengthens my faith. No matter how insurmountable a problem may appear, God is bigger and able to help me withstand the pressure.

Intimacy with God taught me, when doubts arise, to meditate on scriptures, pray, and praise Him in advance for aligning my mind with His truth. Most importantly, wait upon the Lord and listen for instruction.

Intimacy with God made me more grateful for journaling. He illuminates a word or thought in my mind to increase my faith. The recording of His messages to me becomes tangible evidence of my encounters with God.

Applying the lessons learned in my journey will be a continual process. Discovering God's plan for my life to be ready for service as a dance educator, liturgical dancer, intercessor, chaplain, or volunteer is evidence of His grace to transform my thinking.

I trust and pray that anyone who wants to live a victorious, abundant life will invest the time to develop an intimate relationship with God. *Dancing Through the Doubt* was written to help you learn ways to overcome personal obstacles, discover your God-given purpose, and believe what God has to say about you. Trust the process of transformation, and remember, you do not have to be perfect to be used by God.

Cited Sources

The Bible. King James Version, Zondervan, 1994.

The Bible. New International Version, Zondervan, 1985.

Broadus, Monie D. *God's Unchanging Hands*. Monie Broadus, 2009.

Meyer, Joyce. *Battlefield of the Mind: Winning the Battle in Your Mind*. Hachette/Word of Christ Publishing, 2015.

National Liturgical Dance Network. nldnglobal.org.

Overeaters Anonymous. overeaters.org.

Ministry Of Movement

www.ingramcontent.com/pod-product-compliance
Lightning Source LLC
Chambersburg PA
CBHW071743040426
42446CB00012B/2454